~This~

Book Belongs

~To~

Rianna

26/6/06

~The~
Baby
~and~
Toddler
Treasury

~THE~
BABY
~AND~
TODDLER
TREASURY

VIKING

Published by the Penguin Group
Penguin Books Ltd, 27 Wrights Lane, London W8 5TZ, England
Penguin Putnam Inc., 375 Hudson Street, New York, New York 10014, USA
Penguin Books Australia Ltd, Ringwood, Victoria, Australia
Penguin Books Canada Ltd, 10 Alcorn Avenue, Toronto, Ontario, Canada M4V 3B2
Penguin Books India (P) Ltd, 11 Community Centre, Panchsheel Park, New Delhi – 110 017, India
Penguin Books (NZ) Ltd, Cnr Rosedale and Airborne Roads, Albany, Auckland, New Zealand
Penguin Books (South Africa) (Pty) Ltd, 5 Watkins Street, Denver Ext 4, Johannesburg 2094, South Africa

On the World Wide Web at: www.penguin.com

Penguin Books Ltd, Registered Offices: Harmondsworth, Middlesex, England

First published as *The Puffin Baby and Toddler Treasury* by Viking 1998
This abridged edition published as *The Baby and Toddler Treasury* 2000
5 7 9 10 8 6 4

British Library Cataloguing in Publication Data
A CIP catalogue record for this book is available from the British Library

ISBN 0–670–89350–1

CONTENTS

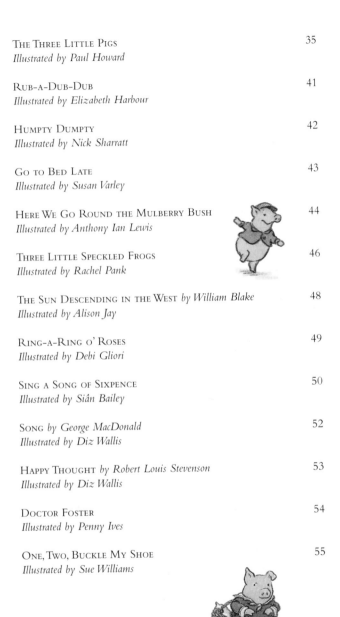

Hey Diddle Diddle

Hey diddle diddle,
The cat and the fiddle,
The cow jumped over the moon;
The little dog laughed
To see such sport,
And the dish ran away with the spoon.

LITTLE MISS MUFFET

Little Miss Muffet
Sat on a tuffet,
Eating her curds and whey;
There came a big spider,
Who sat down beside her
And frightened Miss Muffet away.

OLD MACDONALD HAD A FARM

Old Macdonald had a farm,
E-I-E-I-O!
And on that farm he had some cows,
E-I-E-I-O!
With a moo-moo here,
And a moo-moo there,
Here a moo, there a moo, everywhere a moo-moo,
Old Macdonald had a farm,
E-I-E-I-O!

Old Macdonald had a farm,
E-I-E-I-O!
And on that farm he had some sheep,
E-I-E-I-O!
With a baa-baa here,
And a baa-baa there,
Here a baa, there a baa, everywhere a baa-baa,
With a moo-moo here,
And a moo-moo there,
Here a moo, there a moo, everywhere a moo-moo,
Old Macdonald had a farm,
E-I-E-I-O!

Old Macdonald had a farm,

E-I-E-I-O!

And on that farm he had some ducks,

E-I-E-I-O!

With a quack-quack here,

And a quack-quack there,

Here a quack, there a quack, everywhere a quack-quack,

With a baa-baa here,

And a baa-baa there,

Here a baa, there a baa, everywhere a baa-baa,

With a moo-moo here,

And a moo-moo there,

Here a moo, there a moo, everywhere a moo-moo,

Old Macdonald had a farm,

E-I-E-I-O!

Old Macdonald had a farm,

E-I-E-I-O!

And on that farm he had some hens,

E-I-E-I-O!

With a cluck-cluck here,

And a cluck-cluck there,

Here a cluck, there a cluck, everywhere a cluck-cluck,

With a quack-quack here,

And a quack-quack there,

Here a quack, there a quack, everywhere a quack-quack,
With a baa-baa here,
And a baa-baa there,
Here a baa, there a baa, everywhere a baa-baa,
With a moo-moo here,
And a moo-moo there,
Here a moo, there a moo, everywhere a moo-moo,
Old Macdonald had a farm,
E-I-E-I-O!

Hickory, Dickory, Dock

Hickory, dickory, dock,
The mouse ran up the clock.
The clock struck one,
The mouse ran down,
Hickory, dickory, dock.

POLLY PUT THE KETTLE ON

Polly put the kettle on,
Polly put the kettle on,
Polly put the kettle on,
We'll all have tea.

Sukey take it off again,
Sukey take it off again,
Sukey take it off again,
They've all gone away.

PAT-A-CAKE, PAT-A-CAKE

Pat-a-cake, pat-a-cake, baker's man,
Bake me a cake as fast as you can;
Pat it and prick it, and mark it with B,
Put it in the oven for Baby and me.

Spot's First Picnic

Eric Hill

"They'll be here any minute, Mum!" Spot was going on his first picnic with Tom, Helen and Steve, and he was very excited.

He squeezed three jam sandwiches into his backpack. "I hope I haven't forgotten anything," said Spot as he licked his sticky paws.
Then he had an idea.

"Just what we need for our picnic!"
shouted Spot. And before Sally could stop
him, Spot had pulled the tablecloth off the
table – and everything with it. *Crash!*

A knock at the door saved Spot from getting into more trouble.

"Your friends are here, Spot," Sally called. Spot rushed to the door.

"Oh, great! Let's go. 'Bye, Mum!"

Sally looked up at the sky. It was cloudy. "Be careful," she told them. "And come back if it rains."

"Don't worry," said Helen. "I'll be in charge."

They climbed up a hill and Spot pointed to a small wood on the other side.

"Let's go there," he said. "I know where there's a stream and a big tree we can sit under for our picnic. Come on. I'll race you to the stream!"

Spot got there first. Steve was second and Helen came in third.

Tom panted up last, but when he saw the water, he was the first one in. *Splash!*

Aaahh!

"It was silly of you to jump in like that, Tom," Helen scolded. "You might have hurt yourself."

"Well, I didn't," said Tom. "I'm cool now. Let's go and eat."

Spot, Helen and Steve crossed the stream on stepping stones.

Spot put down the tablecloth and unpacked the food.

They had just started to eat when it began to rain.

"Quick, everyone," Helen shouted. "Put the tablecloth over the branch and make a tent."

It was cosy and dry under the tablecloth, but Steve stayed outside.

"It's only a shower," he said as he climbed up on a branch.

Suddenly Spot heard Steve shout, "Ooops!" and the tent began to shake.

Then everything went dark.

Steve had slipped off the branch and pulled the tent down on top of everyone.

"That's the end of our picnic," moaned Spot.

"It's all your fault, Steve," Helen complained. "You and your silly monkey tricks."

"We may as well go home," said Spot.

They packed up and started back across the stream. But the stones were slippery from the rain and Helen lost her balance.

"Help!" she cried. They all tried to catch Helen, but she fell and pulled everyone into the water with her.

What a mess! Spot looked around and laughed. "That was your fault, Helen. You and your silly balancing tricks!"
Everyone started giggling, and Helen laughed too.
"Wait until Mum sees us," Spot said.

Sally had a surprise ready for them when they got home.

"I knew you'd come back wet and hungry so I made you an indoor picnic."

"Thanks, Mum!" said Spot. "We are starving. We didn't mind getting wet at all, but we did mind eating soggy sandwiches!"

Thanks, Mum.

If You're Happy and You Know It, Clap Your Hands

*I*f you're happy and you know it, clap your hands.
If you're happy and you know it, clap your hands.
If you're happy and you know it and you surely want to show it,
If you're happy and you know it, clap your hands.

If you're happy and you know it, nod your head.
If you're happy and you know it, nod your head.
If you're happy and you know it and you surely want to show it,
If you're happy and you know it, nod your head.

If you're happy and you know it, stamp your feet.
If you're happy and you know it, stamp your feet.
If you're happy and you know it and you surely want to show it,
If you're happy and you know it, stamp your feet.

If you're happy and you know it, say "we are".
If you're happy and you know it, say "we are".
If you're happy and you know it and you surely want to show it,
If you're happy and you know it, say "we are".

If you're happy and you know it, do all four.
If you're happy and you know it, do all four.
If you're happy and you know it and you surely want to show it,
If you're happy and you know it, do all four.

INCY WINCY SPIDER

Incy Wincy spider climbed up the water spout
Down came the rain and washed the spider out.
Out came the sunshine and dried up all the rain,
So Incy Wincy spider climbed up the spout again.

It's Raining, It's Pouring

It's raining, it's pouring,
The old man is snoring;
He went to bed and bumped his head
And couldn't get up in the morning!

LITTLE BO PEEP

Little Bo Peep has lost her sheep
And doesn't know where to find them.
Leave them alone and they'll come home
Bringing their tails behind them.

THE THREE LITTLE PIGS

O nce upon a time there were three little pigs who lived in a very small house with their mother.

One day their mother gathered them all together and said, "It is time that you left our little house and built your own homes."

The three little pigs said goodbye to their mother and as they set off down the road she called after them, "Beware the wolf doesn't catch you and eat you!"

Soon they met a man who was carrying some straw.

"May I have some of your straw?" said the first

little pig. "I want to build a straw house for myself."

So the man gave the first little pig some straw to build a house.

"Now I am sure to be safe from the wolf," said the first little pig.

The other two little pigs went on their way, and soon they met a man who was carrying some sticks.

"May I have some of your sticks?" said the second little pig. "I want to build a wooden house for myself."

So the man gave the second little pig some sticks to build a house.

"Now I am sure to be safe from the wolf," said the second little pig.

The third little pig continued down the road by himself. Soon he met a man who was carrying some bricks.

"May I have some of your bricks?" said the third little pig. "I want to build a brick house for myself."

So the man gave the third little pig some bricks to build a house.

"Now I am
sure to be safe
from the wolf,"
said the third
little pig.

The very next
day the wolf came to the first little pig's house of
straw.

"Little pig, little pig, let me come in," cried the
wolf.

But the first little pig replied, "No, not by the hair
of my chinny chin chin. You may not come in."

"Then I'll huff and I'll puff and I'll blow your
house down!" said the wolf.

So he huffed and he puffed and he huffed and he
puffed. The house of straw fell to pieces, and the wolf
ate up the first little pig.

The next day the wolf came to the second little
pig's house of sticks. "Little pig, little pig, let me
come in," he cried.

But the second little pig replied, "No, not by the
hair of my chinny chin chin. You may not come in."

"Then I'll huff and I'll puff and I'll blow your

house down!" said the wolf.
So he huffed and he
puffed and he huffed
and he puffed.
The house of
sticks fell to pieces, and the wolf
ate up the second little pig.

The next day the wolf came to
the third little pig's house of bricks. "Little pig, little
pig, let me come in," he cried.

But the third little pig replied, "No, not by the hair
of my chinny chin chin. You may not come in."

"Then I'll huff and I'll puff and I'll blow your
house down!" said the wolf.

So he huffed and he puffed and he huffed and he
puffed. But the steadfast house of bricks did *not* fall
down!

The wolf was very annoyed but then he had an
idea. "Be ready at six o'clock tomorrow morning,
little pig, and I shall take you to Farmer Jones's field
to find some delicious truffles."

The little pig said that he would be ready at six
o'clock. But the little pig was very clever and he

knew that the wolf really wanted to eat him. So the next morning he set off an hour earlier at *five* o'clock. The little pig ran all the way to Farmer Jones's field, filled his basket with truffles and hurried home.

When the wolf arrived at the pig's house to find he'd been tricked, he was very cross.

But then the wolf had another idea. "Be ready at five o'clock tomorrow morning," he said to the little pig, "and I shall take you to Farmer Edwards's oak tree to gather some tasty acorns."

The little pig said that he would be ready at five o'clock. But instead, he set off at *four* o'clock the next morning. He ran all the way to Farmer Edwards's oak tree. He had already climbed to the top of the tree and begun to collect acorns when the wolf found him there.

The little pig saw the wolf coming and he threw an acorn as far as he could. The wolf ran after it. In a flash, the little pig jumped down from the tree and raced home as fast as he could.

When the wolf found out that he had been outwitted again, he

was furious. He went to the little pig's house and banged on the door.

"Little pig, little pig," he cried, "I am going to climb down your chimney and eat you up! *You won't escape me this time!*"

The little pig was very, very frightened indeed. What could he do? He thought and thought and then he had an idea. He hurriedly put a huge pot of water on the fire to boil and waited.

The wolf clambered awkwardly down the chimney. "I'm coming to get you, little pig!" the wolf yelled in triumph. But as there was no lid on the little pig's pot, the wolf tumbled with a splash right into the boiling water.

And that was the end of the wolf!

RUB-A-DUB-DUB

Rub-a-dub-dub,
Three men in a tub,
And who do you think they are?
The butcher, the baker,
The candlestick maker;
Turn 'em out, knaves all three!

HUMPTY DUMPTY

Humpty Dumpty sat on the wall,
Humpty Dumpty had a great fall.
All the King's horses and all the King's men
Couldn't put Humpty together again.

GO TO BED LATE

Go to bed late
Stay very small,
Go to bed early
Grow very tall.

Here We Go Round
the Mulberry Bush

Here we go round the mulberry bush,
The mulberry bush, the mulberry bush,
Here we go round the mulberry bush,
On a cold and frosty morning.

This is the way we wash our hands,
Wash our hands, wash our hands,
This is the way we wash our hands,
On a cold and frosty morning.

This is the way we brush our hair,
Brush our hair, brush our hair,
This is the way we brush our hair,
On a cold and frosty morning.

This is the way we go to school,
Go to school, go to school,
This is the way we go to school,
On a cold and frosty morning.

This is the way we wave bye-bye,
Wave bye-bye, wave bye-bye,
This is the way we wave bye-bye,
On a cold and frosty morning.

Three Little Speckled Frogs

Three little speckled frogs
Sat on a speckled log
Eating a most delicious lunch – yum yum!
One jumped into the pool
Where it was nice and cool,
Then there were two green speckled frogs – glub glub!

Two little speckled frogs
Sat on a speckled log
Eating a most delicious lunch – yum yum!
One jumped into the pool
Where it was nice and cool,
Then there was one green speckled frog – glub glub!

One little speckled frog
Sat on a speckled log
Eating a most delicious lunch – yum yum!
She jumped into the pool
Where it was nice and cool,
Then there were no green speckled frogs – glub glub!

THE SUN DESCENDING
IN THE WEST

The sun descending in the west
The evening star does shine,
The birds are silent in their nest
And I must seek for mine,
The moon like a flower,
In heaven's high bower,
With silent delight
Sits and smiles on the night.

William Blake

Ring-a-Ring o' Roses

Ring-a-ring o' roses,
A pocket full of posies.
A-tishoo! A-tishoo!
We all fall down.

Sing a Song of Sixpence

Sing a song of sixpence,
A pocket full of rye;
Four-and-twenty blackbirds
Baked in a pie.
When the pie was opened
The birds began to sing;
Wasn't that a dainty dish
To set before the King?

The King was in his counting house
Counting out his money;
The Queen was in the parlour
Eating bread and honey;
The maid was in the garden
Hanging out the clothes,
When down flew a blackbird
And pecked off her nose.

Song

Where did you come from, baby dear?
  Out of everywhere into here.

Where did you get your eyes so blue?
  Out of the sky as I came through.

Where did you get that little tear?
  I found it waiting when I got here.

What makes your forehead so smooth and high?
  A soft hand stroked it as I went by.

What makes your cheek like a warm white rose?
  I saw something better than anyone knows.

George MacDonald

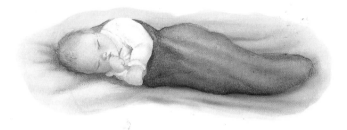

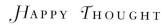

Happy Thought

The world is so full
of a number of things,
I'm sure we should all
be as happy as kings.

Robert Louis Stevenson

Doctor Foster

Doctor Foster went to Gloucester
In a shower of rain;
He stepped in a puddle,
Right up to his middle,
And never went there again.

ONE, TWO, BUCKLE MY SHOE

One, two,
Buckle my shoe;
Three, four,
Knock at the door;
Five, six,
Pick up sticks;
Seven, eight,
Lay them straight;
Nine, ten,
A big fat hen;
Eleven, twelve,
Dig and delve;
Thirteen, fourteen,
Maids a-courting;
Fifteen, sixteen,
Maids in the kitchen;
Seventeen, eighteen,
Maids in waiting;
Nineteen, twenty,
My plate's empty.

WEE WILLIE WINKIE

Wee Willie Winkie runs through the town,
Upstairs and downstairs in his nightgown,
Rapping at the window, crying through the lock,
Are the children in their beds?
For now it's eight o'clock.

Goldilocks
AND THE
Three Bears

Once upon a time, there were three bears who lived in a cosy cottage with a little wooden door and shutters, right in the middle of the big, dark forest.

There was great big Father Bear, who was very fond of eating and sleeping. And there was medium-sized Mother Bear, who was very merry and wise. And there was little tiny Baby Bear, who sometimes cried, but then, after all, he was a very little bear.

One sunny morning, Mother Bear made a big pot of porridge for breakfast. She put it into three bowls and placed them on the kitchen table.

"That looks good," said Father Bear.

"It is good," said Mother Bear.

"Yum, yum," said Baby Bear.

But when they tasted it the three bears discovered that the porridge was much, much too hot to eat.

"We will leave it to cool down while we go out for our early morning walk," said Father Bear. "When we come back, it will be ready to eat." So off they went into the forest.

On the edge of the forest there lived a very naughty, mischievous little girl. She was called Goldilocks because she had long, golden hair down to her waist.

That morning Goldilocks's mother told her to go out into the forest and play.

"But don't go too far!" she said. "And don't get into mischief!"

But naughty Goldilocks went right into the heart of the forest, and there she came across the three bears' pretty little cottage.

"Oh, what a sweet little house! And the door is wide open. I'll just have a peep inside," she said to herself.

So she tiptoed up to the door and, seeing that no one was there, she stepped into the kitchen.

As soon as she saw the porridge on the table, Goldilocks rushed over to taste it. "I do feel hungry, and it smells so delicious," she said. So she picked up a big spoon and dipped it into Father Bear's bowl. "I'll just have a few spoonfuls," she said to herself.

But the porridge in Father Bear's big bowl was still too hot. And when she tried the porridge in Mother Bear's medium-sized bowl she found that was too lumpy.

At last she tried Baby Bear's porridge. It wasn't too hot. It wasn't too lumpy. It was just right! Goldilocks ate up every spoonful!

After that, Goldilocks felt very full. "I need to sit down!" she said. So she climbed up into Father Bear's chair. But it was much too high for her.

Then she sat in Mother Bear's medium-sized chair. "This one is much too hard!" she grumbled.

At last she found Baby Bear's tiny little chair with the letters BB carved into the

back of it. It wasn't too high. It wasn't
too hard. It was just right!

Goldilocks curled up happily
in Baby Bear's chair. But she
was far too heavy for such a
little chair. With a terrible crash,
the legs collapsed and the back fell off, and
Goldilocks found herself sitting on the floor.

"Fiddlesticks!" said Goldilocks. "None of these
chairs is any good. I shall have to find somewhere to
lie down."

And she marched straight upstairs to the bedroom.
She tried lying down in Father Bear's big bed, but
that was far too hard.

Then she tried lying down in Mother Bear's
medium-sized bed, but that was far too soft!

So she lay down on Baby Bear's bed. It wasn't too
hard. It wasn't too soft. It was just right!

"Oh! This is very comfortable," sighed Goldilocks,
snuggling into the little bed. And she fell asleep right
away!

Just then the three bears arrived home hungry
from their early morning walk.

"I'm ready for my breakfast *right this minute*," said Father Bear as they stepped through the front door. But when he sat down at the table he cried out in surprise, "Someone's been eating my porridge!"

"And someone's been eating *my* porridge," said Mother Bear. "I wonder why they didn't finish it?" she said, looking at her bowl.

"They must have liked mine!" cried Baby Bear, holding out his empty bowl. "Someone's been eating my porridge, and they've eaten all of it!" And tears sprang to his eyes.

"Look!" said Father Bear, pointing at his big chair. "Someone's been sitting in my chair!"

"And someone's been sitting in *my* chair," said Mother Bear.

"Someone's been sitting in my chair," wailed poor little Baby Bear, "and they've broken it all to pieces!"

"There, there, poor little Baby Bear," soothed

Mother Bear, "we'll get to the bottom of this."

The three bears began to search the house. They went upstairs to look around. "Someone's been sleeping in my bed!" said Father Bear.

"And someone's been sleeping in *my* bed," cried Mother Bear, "and they've left it in quite a mess!"

"Oh!" whimpered Baby Bear. "Someone's been sleeping in my bed and she's *still there!*" And he burst into tears.

At the sound of Baby Bear's voice, Goldilocks woke up with a start. The first thing she saw was Father Bear, looking very cross and baring his sharp teeth. And then she saw Mother Bear with her arms folded and tapping her foot. And then she saw Baby Bear weeping into his handkerchief. Goldilocks jumped up in fright. She ran down the stairs and out of the house and into the forest as fast as her legs could carry her.

"I don't think that naughty little girl will trouble us again," said Father Bear, smiling.

And she never, ever did.

THE WHEELS ON THE BUS

The wheels on the bus go round and round
Round and round
Round and round
The wheels on the bus go round and round
All day long.

The horn on the bus goes beep beep beep
Beep beep beep
Beep beep beep
The horn on the bus goes beep beep beep
All day long.

The lights on the bus go blink blink blink
Blink blink blink
Blink blink blink
The lights on the bus go blink blink blink
All day long.

The doors on the bus, they open and shut
Open and shut
Open and shut
The doors on the bus, they open and shut
All day long.

The babies on the bus go wah–wah–wah
Wah–wah–wah
Wah–wah–wah
The babies on the bus go wah–wah–wah
All day long.

The mummies on the bus go shh–shh–shh
Shh–shh–shh
Shh–shh–shh
The mummies on the bus go shh–shh–shh
All day long.

But the children on the bus go up and down
Up and down
Up and down
The children on the bus go up and down
All day long!

One, Two, Three, Four, Five

One, two, three, four, five,
Once I caught a fish alive,
Six, seven, eight, nine, ten,
Then I let it go again.
Why did you let it go?
Because it bit my finger so.
Which finger did it bite?
The little finger on the right.

The North Wind Doth Blow

The north wind doth blow,
And we shall have snow,
And what will poor Robin do then,
Poor thing?
He'll sit in a barn,
And keep himself warm,
And hide his head under his wing,
Poor thing.

STAR LIGHT, STAR BRIGHT

Star light, star bright,
First star I see tonight,
Wish I may,
Wish I might,
Have the wish I wish tonight.

Pussy-cat, Pussy-cat

Pussy-cat, pussy-cat, where have you been?
I've been up to London to visit the Queen.
Pussy-cat, pussy-cat, what did you there?
I frightened a little mouse under her chair.

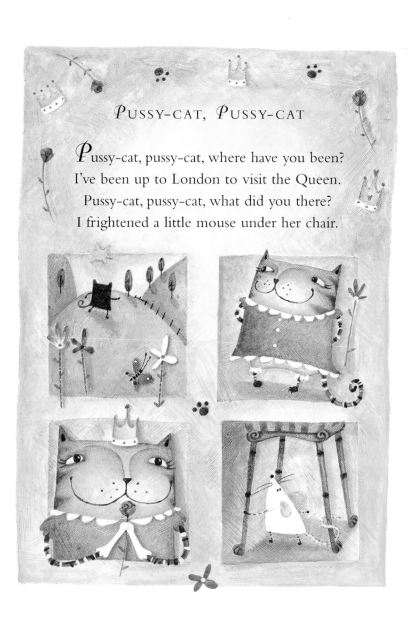

Baa, Baa, Black Sheep

Baa, Baa, black sheep,
Have you any wool?
Yes, sir, yes, sir,
Three bags full;
One for the master,
And one for the dame,
And one for the little boy
Who lives down the lane.

I Love Little Pussy

I love little pussy,
Her coat is so warm,
And if I don't hurt her
She'll do me no harm.
So I'll not pull her tail,
Nor drive her away,
But pussy and I
Very gently will play.
She shall sit by my side,
And I'll give her some food;
And pussy will love me
Because I am good.

OLD KING COLE

Old King Cole
Was a merry old soul,
And a merry old soul was he;
He called for his pipe,
And he called for his bowl,
And he called for his fiddlers three.

Every fiddler he had a fiddle,
And a very fine fiddle had he;
Oh, there's none so rare
As can compare
With King Cole and his fiddlers three.

73

BED IN SUMMER

*I*n winter I get up at night
And dress by yellow candle-light.
In summer, quite the other way,
    I have to go to bed by day.

    I have to go to bed and see
The birds still hopping on the tree,
Or hear the grown-up people's feet
Still going past me in the street.

And does it not seem hard to you,
When all the sky is clear and blue,
And I should like so much to play,
    To have to go to bed by day?

Robert Louis Stevenson

SPRING GOES,
SUMMER COMES

The little darling, Spring,
Has run away;
The sunshine grew too hot for her to stay.

She kissed her sister, Summer,
And she said:
"When I am gone, you must be queen instead."

Now reigns the Lady Summer,
Round whose feet
A thousand fairies flock with blossoms sweet.

Cicely Mary Barker

THREE LITTLE MONKEYS

Three little monkeys jumping on the bed
One fell off and bumped his head.
Mummy called the doctor and the doctor said,
"No more monkeys jumping on the bed!"

Two little monkeys jumping on the bed
One fell off and bumped his head.
Mummy called the doctor and the doctor said,
"No more monkeys jumping on the bed!"

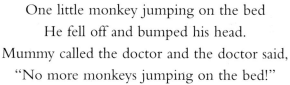One little monkey jumping on the bed
He fell off and bumped his head.
Mummy called the doctor and the doctor said,
"No more monkeys jumping on the bed!"

I'm a Little Teapot

I'm a little teapot,
Short and stout,
Here's my handle,
Here's my spout.
When the kettle's boiling
Hear me shout:
Tip me up
And pour me out!

I Had a Little Nut Tree

I had a little nut tree,
Nothing would it bear
But a silver nutmeg
And a golden pear;
The King of Spain's daughter
Came to visit me,
And all for the sake
Of my little nut tree.

THIS LITTLE PIGGY

This little piggy went to market;
This little piggy stayed at home;
This little piggy had roast beef;
This little piggy had none;
And this little piggy cried, "Wee! Wee! Wee!"
All the way home.

LITTLE BOY BLUE

Little Boy Blue,
Come blow your horn,
The sheep's in the meadow,
The cow's in the corn.
Where is the boy
Who looks after the sheep?
He's under a haystack
Fast asleep.
Will you wake him?
No, not I,
For if I do,
He's sure to cry.

LONDON BRIDGE IS FALLING DOWN

London Bridge is falling down,
Falling down, falling down,
London Bridge is falling down,
My fair lady.

Build it up with wood and clay,
Wood and clay, wood and clay,
Build it up with wood and clay,
My fair lady.

Wood and clay will wash away,
Wash away, wash away,
Wood and clay will wash away,
My fair lady.

Build it up with bricks and mortar,
Bricks and mortar, bricks and mortar,
Build it up with bricks and mortar,
My fair lady.

Bricks and mortar will not stay,
Will not stay, will not stay,
Bricks and mortar will not stay,
My fair lady.

Build it up with iron and steel,
Iron and steel, iron and steel,
Build it up with iron and steel,
My fair lady.

Iron and steel will bend and bow,
Bend and bow, bend and bow,
Iron and steel will bend and bow,
My fair lady.

Build it up with silver and gold,
Silver and gold, silver and gold,
Build it up with silver and gold,
My fair lady.

Silver and gold will be stolen away,
Stolen away, stolen away,
Silver and gold will be stolen away,
My fair lady.

Brahms's Lullaby

Lullaby and goodnight
With rosy bed light,
With down overspread
Is baby's sweet bed.

Lay you down now and rest,
May your slumbers be blest,
Lay you down now and rest,
May your slumbers be blest.

Johannes Brahms

The
Snowman

The original pictures, with words, by
Raymond Briggs

In the morning James woke to see snow falling. He
ran into the garden as fast as he could and started to
make a snowman. He gave him a scarf and a hat, a
tangerine for a nose, and lumps of coal for his buttons
and his eyes.

What a wonderful snowman he was! James could not go to sleep because he was thinking about him.

In the middle of the night he crept down to see the snowman again.

Then suddenly . . . the snowman *moved*!

"Come in," said James. "But you must be very quiet."

The snowman was amazed by everything he saw.

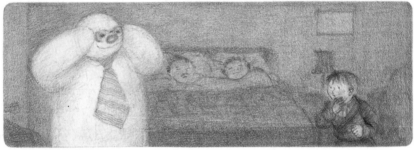

They even went into James's mother and father's bedroom and the snowman dressed up in their clothes.

Suddenly, the snowman took James by the hand and ran out of the house, across the snow and up, up into the air.

They were flying!

James and the snowman flew for miles through the cold, moonlight air.

Then they landed gently on the snow, home safe in the garden.

James gave the snowman a hug.

Then he said good night and went indoors.

In the morning he was woken up by bright sunlight
shining on his face. He must see the snowman again!
James ran out of his room, down the stairs, across the
living room, past his mother and father,

95

and into the garden.

Rock-a-Bye, Baby

Rock-a-bye, baby, on the tree top;
When the wind blows, the cradle will rock;
When the bough bends, the cradle will fall;
Down will come baby, cradle and all.

A Baby-Sermon

The lightning and thunder
They go and they come;
But the stars and the stillness
Are always at home.

George MacDonald

DIDDLE, DIDDLE DUMPLING

Diddle, diddle dumpling,
   my son John,
Went to bed with
   his trousers on;
One shoe off
and one shoe on,
Diddle, diddle dumpling,
   my son John.

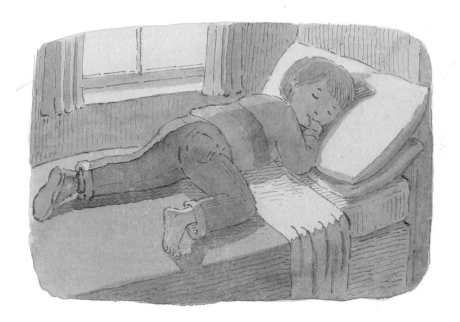

Pop Goes the Weasel

Half a pound of tuppenny rice,
Half a pound of treacle,
That's the way the money goes,
Pop goes the weasel!

Up and down the city road,
In and out the eagle,
That's the way the money goes,
Pop goes the weasel!

Every night when I go out,
The monkey's on the table,
Take a stick and knock it off,
Pop goes the weasel!

A penny for a ball of thread,
Another for a needle,
That's the way the money goes,
Pop goes the weasel!

All around the cobbler's bench,
The monkey chased the people;
The donkey thought 'twas all in fun,
Pop goes the weasel!

Lavender's Blue, Dilly, Dilly

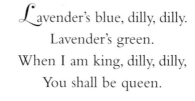

Lavender's blue, dilly, dilly.
Lavender's green.
When I am king, dilly, dilly,
You shall be queen.

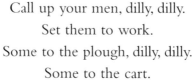

Call up your men, dilly, dilly.
Set them to work.
Some to the plough, dilly, dilly.
Some to the cart.

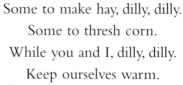

Some to make hay, dilly, dilly.
Some to thresh corn.
While you and I, dilly, dilly.
Keep ourselves warm.

HEADS AND SHOULDERS

Heads and shoulders, knees and toes, knees and toes,
Heads and shoulders, knees and toes, knees and toes,
And eyes and ears and mouth and nose,
Heads and shoulders, knees and toes, knees and toes.

The Grand Old Duke of York

Oh, the grand old Duke of York,
He had ten thousand men;
He marched them up to the top of the hill,
And he marched them down again.
And when they were up, they were up,
And when they were down, they were down,
And when they were only halfway up,
They were neither up nor down.

THE
UGLY
DUCKLING

Based on the story by Hans Christian Andersen

Once upon a time, there was a duck. She lived on a farm and spent her days happily scratching for food in the farmyard with the other ducks and the chickens and swimming in the duckpond.

But one day, the duck felt restless. She couldn't settle to swimming in the pond or scratching for food as usual. "I know what I want!" she cried. "I want to lay some eggs!"

She didn't want all the other ducks to know, so she scrambled out under the farmyard gate and into the field beyond. She waddled off down to the river bank, and found a nice, quiet place where the grass was thick and lush and the rushes grew tall. "This is just the spot to build a nest. My eggs will be nice and safe here," she said.

Once the duck had laid her eggs, she had to sit on them to keep them warm for many days. Every so often, she left the nest to go down to the river for some food and a drink of water, but she always hurried back to her eggs as fast as she could.

Finally, the big day arrived – the eggs were ready to hatch! First one, then two, three, four chicks pecked their way out through the eggshell. The duck was so thrilled, she couldn't help quacking with excitement, "Oh, how little and yellow and beautiful you are! I shall be the envy of all the other ducks in the farmyard!"

But the fifth chick was different. He wasn't little or yellow. He was big and grey, and when he finally

chipped his way out of the egg his mother was
horrified. "Oh my goodness!" she sobbed. "What a
very *ugly* duckling you are!"

The next day the mother duck took the five little
chicks down to the river to teach them how to
swim, then it was time to go back to the farmyard.
Proudly, the mother duck introduced her new brood,
and the other ducks agreed that the four little yellow
chicks were very beautiful indeed.

But none of them liked the fifth chick at all. "He's
so big!" "And grey!" "And *ugly*!" they said.

The ugly duckling tried to make friends, but no
one would play with him or talk to him, not even
his brothers and sisters. They all just
laughed at him and said unkind things.

So he decided to run away. Early
one morning, he squeezed
under the gate and ran down
to the river. Then he swam
and swam and swam
until he could swim

ho ho

ha ha

no more. Night was falling and he was miles away from home in the middle of a dark wood. He climbed out on to the river bank. It was cold and the poor little ugly duckling was frightened and lonely.

Then, as he huddled himself up under some leaves, he heard voices calling from the sky. Looking up, he saw some beautiful white swans flying overhead. "How lovely they are!" he thought to himself. "If only I could be like them!" And he fell fast asleep.

The next day, the ugly duckling was looking for food on the river, when some wild ducks came swimming up. "What an ugly duckling you are!" they said. "You can't stay here!" They pecked him with their sharp beaks until he ran away.

Soon, he was hopelessly lost in the wood. Rain was falling and the little ugly duckling was weak with hunger and tiredness, when he came across a cottage. There was a gap under the door just big enough for him to squeeze through.

hello there!

Inside, he found a lovely warm fire with a cat and a hen and a little old lady in

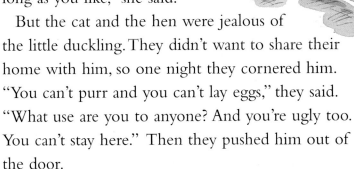

go away!

front of it. The little old
lady gave the duckling
some water to drink and
some corn to eat and a
cosy warm seat in front of
the fire. "You can stay here as
long as you like," she said.

But the cat and the hen were jealous of
the little duckling. They didn't want to share their
home with him, so one night they cornered him.
"You can't purr and you can't lay eggs," they said.
"What use are you to anyone? And you're ugly too.
You can't stay here." Then they pushed him out of
the door.

So the poor little duckling set off on his travels
once more, out on to the great lonely marshland. But
winter was falling, and as the weather got colder and
colder, it grew harder and harder for the duckling to
find food. One morning, a farmer came across the
duckling half frozen on the ice. He took the
duckling home to his wife, who fed him and looked
after him until he was strong again.

But the farmer's children wanted to play with him.

They chased him and pulled his tail, until the duckling had to run away again.

The ugly duckling stayed hidden among the reeds through the rest of the long cold winter, until the spring sunshine fell brightly on the water. Then he stretched his wings and flew up into the sky and over the river.

Down below, he saw three lovely white swans swimming. "Come and join us!" they called. The duckling could hardly believe they were talking to him, but as he flew down, he caught sight of his own reflection in the river. He saw strong white wings and a long white neck and he realized that he wasn't an ugly duckling any more. He was a beautiful swan, just like the ones calling to him, and he would never be lonely again.

HUSH, LITTLE BABY

Hush, little baby, don't say a word,
Papa's going to buy you a mocking bird.

If the mocking bird won't sing,
Papa's going to buy you a diamond ring.

If the diamond ring turns to brass,
Papa's going to buy you a looking glass.

If the looking glass gets broke,
Papa's going to buy you a billy goat.

If that billy goat runs away,
Papa's going to buy you another today.

ROUND AND ROUND THE GARDEN

Round and round the garden
Like a teddy bear,
One step,
Two step,
And tickly under there!

RAIN, RAIN, GO AWAY

*R*ain, rain, go away,
Come again another day.

Dance to Your Daddy

Dance to your daddy,
My little babby,
Dance to your daddy,
My little lamb.

You shall have a fishy
In a little dishy,
You shall have a fishy
When the boat comes in.

Roses are Red

Roses are red,
Violets are blue,
Honey is sweet
And so are you.

THIS IS THE WAY THE LADY RIDES

This is the way the lady rides,
Nim, nim, nim, nim,
This is the way the gentleman rides,
Trim, trim, trim, trim,
This is the way the farmer rides,
Trot, trot, trot, trot,
This is the way the huntsman rides,
A-gallop, a-gallop, a-gallop, a-gallop,
This is the way the old man rides,
Hobbledehoy, hobbledehoy, hobbledehoy,
And down into the ditch!

I See the Moon

I see the moon,
And the moon sees me;
God bless the moon,
And God bless me.

Horsie, Horsie

Horsie, horsie, don't you stop,
Just let your feet go clippetty clop;
Your tail goes swish, and the wheels go round –
Giddy up, you're homeward bound!

THE
GINGERBREAD
MAN

*O*nce upon a time there was a little old woman and a little old man, and they lived all alone. They were very happy together, but they wanted a child and since they had none, they decided to make one out of gingerbread. So one day the little old woman and the little old man made themselves a little gingerbread man, and they put him in the oven to bake.

When the gingerbread man was done, the little old woman opened the oven door and pulled out the pan. Out jumped the little gingerbread man – and

away he ran.
The little old
woman and
the little old
man ran after
him as fast as they
could, but he just
laughed and said, "Run,
run, as fast as you can. You
can't catch me! I'm the
Gingerbread Man!"

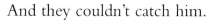

And they couldn't catch him.

The gingerbread man ran on and on until he came
to a cow.

"Stop, little gingerbread man," said the cow. "I
want to eat you."

But the gingerbread man said, "I have run away
from a little old woman and a little old man, and I
can run away from you, too. I can, I can!"

And the cow began to chase the gingerbread man,
but the gingerbread man ran faster, and said, "Run,
run, as fast as you can. You can't catch me! I'm the
Gingerbread Man!"

And the cow couldn't catch him.

The gingerbread man ran on until he came to a horse.

"Please, stop, little gingerbread man," said the horse. "I want to eat you."

And the gingerbread man said, "I have run away from a little old woman, a little old man, and a cow, and I can run away from you, too. I can, I can!"

And the horse began to chase the gingerbread man, but the gingerbread man ran faster and called to the horse, "Run, run, as fast as you can. You can't catch me! I'm the Gingerbread Man!"

And the horse couldn't catch him.

By and by the gingerbread man came to a field full of farmers.

"Stop," said the farmers. "Don't run so fast. We want to eat you."

But the gingerbread man said, "I have run away from a little old woman, a little old man, a cow, and a horse, and I can run away from you, too. I can, I can!"

And the farmers began to chase him, but the gingerbread man ran faster than ever and said, "Run, run, as fast as you can. You can't catch me! I'm the Gingerbread Man!"

And the farmers couldn't catch him.

The gingerbread man ran faster and faster. He ran past a school full of children.

"Stop, little gingerbread man," said the children. "We want to eat you."

But the gingerbread man said, "I have run away from a little old woman, a little old man, a cow, a horse, and a field full of farmers, and I can run away from you, too. I can, I can!"

And the children began to chase him, but the gingerbread man ran faster as he said, "Run, run, as fast as you can. You can't catch me! I'm the Gingerbread Man!"

And the children couldn't catch him.

By this time the gingerbread man was so proud of himself he didn't think anyone could catch him. Pretty soon he saw a fox. The fox looked at him and began to run after him. But the gingerbread man said, "You can't catch me! I have run away from a little old woman, a little old man, a cow, a horse, a field full of farmers, a school full of children, and I can run away from you, too. I can, I can! Run, run, as fast as you can. You can't catch me! I'm the Gingerbread Man!"

"Oh," said the fox, "I do not want to catch you. I only want to help you run away."

Just then the gingerbread man came to a river. He could not swim across, and he had to keep running.

"Jump on my tail," said the fox. "I will take you across."

So the gingerbread man jumped on the fox's tail, and the fox began to swim across the river. When he had gone a little way, he said to the gingerbread man, "You are too heavy on my tail. Jump on my back."

And the gingerbread man did.

The fox swam a little further, and then he said, "I am afraid you will get wet on my back. Jump on my shoulder."

And the gingerbread man did.

In the middle of the river, the fox said, "Oh dear, my shoulder is sinking. Jump on my nose, and I can hold you out of the water."

So the little gingerbread man jumped on the fox's nose, and the fox threw back his head and snapped his sharp teeth.

"Oh dear," said the gingerbread man, "I am a quarter gone!"

Next minute he said, "Now I am half gone!"

And next minute he said, "Oh, my goodness gracious! I am three quarters gone!"

And then the gingerbread man never said anything more at all.

Row, Row, Row Your Boat

Row, row, row your boat,
Gently down the stream.
Merrily, merrily, merrily, merrily;
Life is but a dream.

I SAW A SHIP A-SAILING

I saw a ship a-sailing,
A-sailing on the sea,
And oh, but it was laden
With pretty things for thee!

There were comfits in the cabin,
And apples in the hold;
The sails were made of silk,
And the masts were all of gold.

The four-and-twenty sailors
That stood between the decks
Were four-and-twenty white mice
With chains about their necks.

The captain was a duck
With a packet on his back,
And when the ship began to move
The captain said, "Quack! Quack!"

ACKNOWLEDGEMENTS

The editor and publishers gratefully acknowledge the following for permission to reproduce copyright material in this book:

'Spring Goes, Summer Comes' by Cicely Mary Barker from *Flower Fairies of the Summer* copyright © the Estate of Cicely Mary Barker, 1924, 1944, reproduced by permission of Frederick Warne & Co., illustrations by Cicely Mary Barker copyright © the Estate of Cicely Mary Barker, 1925, 1934, 1940, 1944, 1990, reproduced by permission of Frederick Warne & Co.; revised text from *The Snowman Story Book* by Raymond Briggs, first published by Hamish Hamilton Ltd 1990, revised edition published in the UK in Puffin Books 1992 and in the USA by Random House, Inc. 1990, copyright © Raymond Briggs, 1992, with additional illustrations from *The Snowman*, first published by Hamish Hamilton Ltd 1978 and in the USA by Random House, Inc. 1978, copyright © Raymond Briggs, 1978, reprinted by kind permission of the author and by arrangement with Random House, Inc.; illustrations by Elizabeth Harbour on pages 1, 37 and 176–7 from *A First Picture Book of Nursery Rhymes*, published by Viking 1995, reprinted by kind permission of the illustrator; *Spot's First Picnic* by Eric Hill copyright © Eric Hill, 1987, this presentation 1998, reproduced by permission of Ventura Publishing.

Grateful acknowledgement is made to *This Little Puffin*, compiled by Elizabeth Matterson, first published 1969 by Puffin Books, a publishing division of Penguin Books Ltd, revised edition published 1991. Since its first publication in 1969, *This Little Puffin* has become a classic of its kind. Parents, teachers, child-minders, playgroup leaders and many others have found it an invaluable source of rhymes, songs and games for young children.

Every effort has been made to trace copyright holders, but if there are any omissions the editor and publishers apologize for any copyright transgression and would like to hear from any copyright holders not acknowledged.